fighting temptations

A PERSONAL STUDY GUIDE TO TRUE FREEDOM
FROM ADDICTIONS AND CHARACTER FLAWS

SANDRA ALANWOKO

I dedicate this book to my father, Pastor Sylvester Alanwoko whose memories live on in my heart; my first pastor and mentor

To my mother, Mary for teaching me about the Holy Spirit

To my husband, Inyang Lawrence for being the best team and destiny partner

To my twin sister, Cynthia Alanwoko for being my covenant friend and confidant

To all my siblings, Pastor Favor, Mrs. Blessing, Pastor Emmanuel for always being there to cheer me on

To the All Nations family, Pastor Teresa and Pastor Gordon for being an early inspiration for me

To all my mentors who tirelessly prayed for me and stood by me until… I became.

…and to young people seeking to be free…

Fighting Temptations
A Personal Study Guide to True Freedom From Addictions and Character Flaws

"Lord what is in the mind of the addict?
How would You reach them if You
were here walking with us?"

Sandra Alanwoko Lawrence provides the beginning of a clear answer to
that question. Hope of how to begin the journey and how to allow God to
shape a fresh and new way to think and live.

REV. TERESA SKINNER

foreword

Have you longed for a book to help yourself or a friend overcome addiction and begin to live a victorious life free from the shame and guilt which sin causes?

This book which Sandra has written is honest, transparent and filled with truth. It is direct but not condemning. I believe that the principles laid out in these pages can help many who have found themselves lost in a maze of addiction, sin, shame and bondage which seems too powerful or too hopeless to overcome. This book is a "roadmap" written by someone who found the way out of her own addicting habits and has done a wonderful job of giving her readers a clear pathway to freedom.

I love the sincerity of this book and highly recommend it.

REV. GORDON SKINNER

part one

THE BEGINNING...

the test of will

One of the first strategies that the devil deploys is to test our will. He will always seek to know what the state of your heart is towards God and his command. He looks for any iota of delayed or restrained obedience as well as any headiness towards complete accordance to God's commands (partial obedience).

He tries to bring you to the point where you battle between complete obedience and partial obedience, as soon as he successfully wages this war inside you; he has got some sort of foothold. He finds the person who is seeking his own will an escape route to partial obedience, and then he begins to release his ideas to the willing heart. He starts selling his deceptive ideas and keeps echoing this lie in your heart, "as long as you don't actually do it, if you are only at the brink of it, then you are just fine... you have not disobeyed God."

Be careful of the devil's 'at least', be careful of his subtle ways. The devil never provides any solution; there are no short cuts to righteousness. He goes further to say "God will understand because it will be hard to completely stay away, you know?", "You can just drink a small amount of alcohol", "You can just masturbate at least, you are not doing it with anybody", "You can just kiss her/finger her at least you are not sleeping with her..."

> BE CAREFUL OF THE DEVIL'S 'AT LEAST'
> BE CAREFUL OF HIS SUBTLE WAYS.

If the enemy of your soul finds your heart not willing to obey God completely, he will suggest strategies to disobey God that will not bear any appearance of sin so to get you trapped; like a fish coming for the bait yet ignorant of the hook underneath.

Make up your mind to go through that hard way:

- To stand no matter how hard it might seem
- To stay on God's highway even if you are the only one on that road
- To never look back no matter how tempting the urge to and
- To NEVER turn to the devil's by-ways

the devil's snare

"Has God indeed said, "You shall not eat of every tree of the garden? You will not surely die."

The devil always has a major strategy of subtlety. He tries to get us to have one bite, one trapping bite. It took just one bite to get Adam and Eve out of the Garden of Eden.

What is a snare? It is something deceptively attractive of which one is unaware.

The Bible says that each man is drawn by his own desires (James 1:14-15) . The adversary of our souls is very skillful in the use of his snare. He starts by pushing you strongly in the direction of your desires and likes. He tells you "Don't you like him/her?" "Don't you appreciate the view?" Once he is able to establish a strong force or urge dragging you to that weakness, character flaw or sinful desire, he then moves on to the next strategy.

Once the strong urge is established, the devil goes on to suggest to his victims to "Just take a bite," or rather "Just try it small." "Just try a little bit." He buttresses his point by saying to his victim that he or she can just have **a little** to quench the urge and that is all. He echoes **'the little'** in such a way that it will look so minute and harmless. But, he knows that **'just a little'** compromise is all that he needs to get you down from your throne, given to you by God your father where you are sitting with Jesus in heavenly places. He knows that **'just a little'** compromise is all that he needs to turn a prince into a slave — a slave to sin, guilt and shame. He knows that when you compromise the first time, it becomes easier the next time.

One disobedience can put you on the path of perpetual damnation. Be careful of the devil's strategy.

 Realize that when you keep doing what is wrong, it becomes hard to do right, but when you keep doing what is right it becomes difficult to do what is wrong.

THREE

god is merciful

WITH PRIVILEGES COMES RESPONSIBILITIES

The next strategy or tool in the devil's weaponry is to get you to see that God is merciful and that he understands. He over blows this into a fantastical ideology that sins can go unpunished because of God's mercy.

The Bible tells us not to use grace as a license to sin (Romans 6:15). If you love God, you will protect him from hurt and from heartbreak over and over on the basis of his merciful nature. Yes, God will forgive you, but your heart will start moving farther and farther away from him. You will continue to grieve his spirit and maybe get your conscience seared in that area or aspect.

BE CAREFUL OF THE DEVIL'S 'AT LEAST'
BE CAREFUL OF HIS SUBTLE WAYS.

If you truly love God; you will not allow the devil to wrap you with guilt and shame thus making you lose your confidence before God and his people.

Always remember that the old man grows corrupt (Ephesians 4) and corruption does not happen overnight. I know it is hard to break a pattern, but you have to make up your mind to break free. You must make a personal decision enabled by the Holy Spirit to no longer submit your will to the devil to sin against God and your body. You must say no to his snare and deceptive desire.

With privileges comes responsibilities don't be deceived to think that God's privileges of grace do not come with responsibilities of discipline, self control and temperance on our part. It might look attractive, YES but it is not for you. The fruit may look quite attractive on the outside but inside it is all rotten and bad.

 With privileges comes responsibilities don't be deceived to think that God's privileges of grace do not come with responsibilities of discipline, self control and temperance on our part.

can't help myself

As soon as the devil has gotten his victim to eat the forbidden fruit… (fall into temptation), if you truly love God, your conscience will turn on the **Red Alert.** The devil will then capitalize on the promptings of your conscience to get you to start feeling guilty, worthless and wrapped in shame. He will tell you, "How come you can commit such a sin like this if you love God?" "Are you sure you are a child of God?"

He starts telling you that God is disappointed in you and that God is unhappy with you. His intention is to get you to feel guilty and then walk away from God and walk into his camp. His intention is to get you to believe that God has given up on you and that there is no more room for you in God's mercy.

THAT IS A LIE !!!

God expects his children to come boldly into his throne of Grace and Mercy to obtain mercy and find grace, to help in time of need. (Hebrews 4:16). The enemy of your soul wants you to hide away in shame and guilt like Adam and Eve, when they ate the forbidden fruit from the Garden of Eden. And then they hid away from the presence of God, when God appeared in the evening to have fellowship with them. This is all the enemy of our soul wants, **He wants us to be separated from the father** just as he was separated and thrown down to hell out of heaven. No matter how far you've gone, there is and will always be room at the cross for you. God will always take in any son who returns to him in repentance and truly makes a 180 degree turn back to the father.

If the devil gets his victim to believe that he or she has wronged God and as such has disappointed God, he continues to suggest to you that there is nothing you can do about that weakness. He rather suggests to his victim to accept that weakness as a part of his/her identity.

Resist him and vehemently refuse to accept the blatant lie about your identity no matter how many times you've fallen or you may fall. The moment you accept that weakness as your identity, then, there is barely little that can be done to help you.

A dog cannot be made to swim and a fish cannot be made to walk on land, why? It is not in their nature. They are not configured to do so. If you are a child of God, you are not configured to lustful desires of this elementary life because the **DNA of God runs in you.** It is time to wake up to your true nature and your intended shape.

Refuse to accept the devil's lies that you can't help yourself. You can do all things through Christ who gives you strength (Philippians 4:13).

- **YOU CAN BE FREE**
- **YOU CAN BE DELIVERED!!!**

The moment you accept that weakness as your identity, then, there is barely little that can be done to help you.

Don't accept the lie.

part 2

SOMEWHERE IN THE MIDDLE

the struggle

You can be free, you can be delivered, it all starts in the mind. The wise man said it is called 'mindset' because the mind sets your whole world. This is the reason why more often than not the devil attacks our mind. He knows the battlefield is in the mind, but thanks be to God who gives us the victory through Jesus Christ (1 Corinthians 15:57). We can and we will conquer that battlefield in our mind.

One way to conquer the battles in the mind is to feed the mind with the truth. What you feed a child, will determine how the child will grow. The scripture says "The truth will set you free."

Has the enemy trapped you with lies, has he thrown bullets and more bullets of lies to your mind and it seems he is about to win the battle? It is time to feed your mind with the truth. It is time to starve the flesh of its food, and feed spirit. For the flesh and spirit war against each other (Galatians 5:17). This is an ancient battle and it would not end with you. This battle that is in our mind is always between the flesh and the spirit. Who you feed will be stronger, who you don't feed will be weaker.

A story was told about a man who was good at predicting dog fights, whichever of the two dogs he predicted would win, that dog would win. One day a young boy decided to become his apprentice and learn this act of predicting dog fights. So, he asked his master after he had began his apprenticeship, "Sir, how do you know which dog will win?" The master answered and said, "The that one I want to win, I feed well before the day of the fight, while the one I want to lose; I starve that week."

The same applies to the battle in our mind, if we are tired of losing to the flesh, it is time to starve the flesh and start feeding the spirit. This is the only way to win this ancient battle. It is time to take up the shield of faith and protect our mind from the fiery darts of the evil one. It is also time to take up the sword of the spirit which is the word of God and **fight this good fight of faith.**

To overcome addictions and win this struggle you must start taking a balanced diet. You must eat the word and drink of the spirit through prayer and supplication. You must take spiritual supplements of habitual fasting, this we will discuss more Part Three of this book.

Six facts about temptation

1. **Who:** Temptation can happen to anyone no matter how spiritual and solid one may be. No man is superman.
2. **What:** You can be tempted by anything especially along the line of your own desires. The most common temptation today is sexual, because the opportunity for it is everywhere. We must learn to guard our vulnerable areas with prayer.

3. **When:** Temptation can happen at any time and often when you least expect and when you are most susceptible.

4. **Where:** Temptation can happen anywhere. It will happen in the place you least expect it. Wherever it is, separate yourself from it immediately. If chocolate tempts you, then don't hang around in the candy store.

5. **Why:** The devil tempts us mostly for one major reason, he knows God has great things in store for you and that you have a great destiny ahead. So, he wants you to give it all up for a few moments of false pleasure. Know this, the more you have been given, the more you will be approached by the enemy who will try to take it away from you.

6. **How:** You have to remember that no matter the strategy employed by the enemy, the end point is to bring you down. He always looks out for our weakness and then tempts us with what we are so susceptible to.

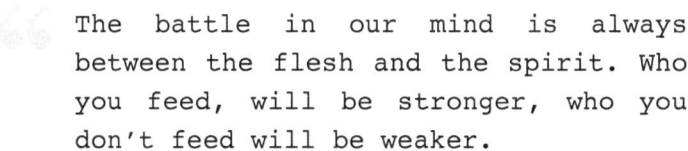

The battle in our mind is always between the flesh and the spirit. Who you feed, will be stronger, who you don't feed will be weaker.

the relapse

This stage, I dare say, is one challenging aspect while trying to break out from an addiction. This chapter, hence, is one that is very passionate to me.

This is because I know what it means to struggle out of an addiction or character flaw, only to fall back in. Most times, coming out after one has fallen, the second time becomes more difficult, intense and twice addictive. More like the sin or evil habit is saying "I've really missed you" or rather, "Welcome back."

Whichever, I'm just trying to paint a mental picture of how twice the struggle the relapse stage can be.

WHAT IS RELAPSE?

Relapse is a situation of deterioration after a period of improvement. In an addiction, relapse is when a person with a past addiction starts doing his or her addictive behavior again after a period of not doing it — known as abstinence.

I know the pain of having to live in guilt and shame all over again, even after you have testified to your mentors that you are finally free. How do you go back to tell them that you've been trapped again? What would they think of you? I know the circle of thoughts that characterize this phase.

Dear reader, if you are reading this and you are probably in this phase right now, **don't feel bad and don't give up.** Though the righteous may fall seven times, he will surely rise again (Proverbs 24:16). This is not a consolation for you to wait until you've fallen seven times, rather it is a wake-up call that you can and **you will** rise up, if only you refuse to accept the present [1]statuesque. There is hope for a tree, even though it be cut down, at the scent of water, it will bounce back (Job 14:7-9). All you need is the **scent of the water** upon your life which represents the presence and the hand of God.

TIPS TO BOUNCING BACK FROM THE RELAPSE STAGE

Total submission: To successfully break free from an addiction, you must successfully submit to God wholly and completely. The scripture says, "Submit yourselves to God, resist the devil and he will flee." (James 4:7) You can only successfully resist the devil when you are fully submitted to God. To come out from the relapse stage, you must not just submit to God but **you must completely give him your all.**

Let the Holy Spirit know that you are tired of your present statuesque, tired of that besetting sin, tired of that weight. It shall come to pass when you are restless, shall the yoke of your brother be broken off your neck. (Genesis 27:40)

You see, there is no deliverance as effective and powerful as personal deliverance. Every anointed man of God can pray for you to be free from any addiction, but until you realize and make up your mind that **you are ready to be free** and to remain free, you cannot be free.

Hence, the first step to total deliverance is total submission.

Total separation: To successfully break free from an addiction, especially at the relapse stage, you must ensure that you become totally separate from sin, self, indulgence and separate unto God. The Bible says that sin shall not have dominion over you (Romans 6:14). This can only happen when you make the decision to stay totally separated unto God.

Total forgiveness: Dear reader, you have to forgive yourself for all the times that you failed. Unforgivingness is a nasty prison that you would not want to live in especially when you are the prison warden against yourself. The Bible tells us to forget the things that are past and press on (Philippians 3:13). You cannot successfully press on with the past dragging you back. Break the chains of the past. The next time the devil tries to remind you that you did this or that, tell him that that was your past, and that you've been set free and delivered and now living a new life in Christ Jesus.

FACTS ABOUT SIN AND ADDICTION

Sin is not something you do and just walk away, the Bible said that sin ties the person that is practicing it with a cord (Proverbs 5:22). Sin ties the victim to itself and draws him back anytime it needs him. **Sin has a seed that yearns and cries out for more of that sin**, The sin draws its practitioner back to commit more sin. All sins have the element of bondage in it, hence, it is safer to stay away from every addiction.

Sin has a bait and a chain that it uses to attract and bind its victims. This slavery is willful. Once you venture in and it traps you, don't say, "We are like fish in the water, we cannot help ourselves." This is a lie. There are some people who have faced the same challenges and overcome them; the Bible lists their names in Hebrews chapter 11.

The Christian race is not a one meter dash, it is a marathon. And you will need endurance and stamina. In this race, you cannot carry any baggage; you need to dismantle every baggage because you will need to run light. The journey is very long and where God is taking you is far.

People who struggle with sin believe that if they work harder they will be free from sin. If you are still struggling with a particular sinful habit; you will notice that it is the same sinful habit that you are still repenting from.

The only way to escape the dominion of sin is through death. You cannot tempt a dead man with fornication or masturbation etc. Why? Because, he is dead.

Don't just see Jesus dying for you, but also see yourself dying with Jesus. This is the revelation of 'co-death.' Where two of you died on the cross.

NOTE: In these end times, the majority of those in the body of Christ that have gone cold or have succumbed to sin and deception, will not pass the test.

EFFECTS OF SIN AND ADDICTION

1. **It has a burden of guilt and depression:** If there is one thing I can say for a certainty, addiction comes with a heavy burden of guilt and depression.

You suddenly lose your joy and you find it hard to speak up, especially in the congregation of friends, leaders and God's people in general.

2. **It brings about lack of faith:** You cannot live in sin and still have great faith. One thing that sin strikes is your faith and confidence. This is because the devil uses sin to rob you of your boldness before your God and Father.

3. **It brings about a feeling of unworthiness**: Sin and addiction will make you feel unworthy of God's grace and blessings, even though they are a free gift of God as a result of the salvation.

4. **It brings about a feeling of helplessness:** Like I explained earlier in the first chapter of this book, sin and addiction lets you believe that there is nothing you can do about the situation; rather to accept it as natural struggle.

5. **It causes a lack of assurance of salvation:** The devil uses sin and addiction to make you question your salvation. You begin to ask, "If I am really born again, I then why am I still struggling with my past life?"

---

1. Footnote
   statuesque: status, position, class

ESCAPE ROUTE

dna transplant

You cannot successfully fight and win against the devil if you are still in his camp. If you are still living in his house, then know this: **You will never win any war against him.**

Even the scriptures say, "A house divided against itself cannot stand." (Mark 3:25) Therefore, if you want to fight your temptations and win, you must be ready to renounce all and everything that belongs to him.

After renouncing the devil, you must **enthrone Jesus Christ** into your life as your Lord and personal Saviour. And you must ask his Holy Spirit to be your guide and your helper. Irrespective of how many times you've done this, it is important you clear the weeds before planting. Thus the need to ask Jesus to rule and reign in your life again.

> Take a moment and ask Jesus to come into your heart. Do not delay or procrastinate on this.

If you have just done this, then you have successfully gone through a DNA transplant. **You have been translated into**

the kingdom of God. You have done away with the bad blood and the **life of Christ now flows through and in you.**

NOTE: A DNA transplant doesn't guarantee or mean that you will not be tempted in the sin that you once did, it only means that this time, because of the life of Christ that now flows through you, **there is a supernatural enabling and urge to please God rather than consent to sin.**

confession and forgiveness

Some may argue that this stage should come before the DNA transplant. True, but for some peculiar reason, I feel it can come after the DNA transplant. This is one phase where the devil held me, and I am sure many others like me, captive.

You have given your life to Christ, you have successfully undergone the DNA transplant, yet the enemy will still want to keep you in his perpetual trap of guilt, and thus make you feel like you can't ever get away. Hence you must open your mouth and speak up as the strength of sin is secrecy. The scriptures say, "Confess your fault one to another." (James 5:16).

When you completely undress for circumcision, the foreskin of your heart will be taken away, and you will become a new creation. The Holy Spirit told me one day, that if the sin is exposed, the devil no longer has a grip on me. And so, I took the bold step and confessed my sins to my spiritual authorities and **I became free indeed.**

When you expose secret sins, the enemy has nothing else to blackmail you with. And, if you believe and know that Jesus has forgiven you, then you can be bold to tell the world of your freedom and deliverance.

> *"For everyone practicing evil hates the light and does not come to the light, lest his deeds should be exposed. But he who does the truth comes to the light, that his deeds may be clearly seen, that they have been done in God."*

JOHN 3:20, 21

> *"Then I heard a loud voice saying in heaven, "Now salvation, and strength, and the kingdom of our God, and the power of His Christ have come, for the accuser of our brethren, who accused them before our God day and night, has been cast down. And they overcame him by the blood of the Lamb and by the word of their testimony, and they did not love their lives to the death."*

REVELATION 12:10, 11

spirit within and spirit upon

You cannot successfully break free from addiction alone. You need both divine and physical assistance, but **most importantly, divine assistance.** The scriptures say "By the strength no man shall prevail." (1 Samuel 2:9). Hence we must "Not lean on our own understanding" (Proverbs 3:5).

After you have invited Jesus to become your Lord, King and Saviour. The next thing you must do is to ask the Holy Spirit to come and have his way in your life. You must ask the Holy Spirit to direct, guide and help you come out of that addiction, character flaw or habit.

THE SPIRIT WITHIN

The Spirit within refers to the indwelling presence of the Holy Spirit. It is the work of the Holy Spirit to produce the fruit of the Spirit. The fruit of the Spirit (Galatians 5:22) talks about the character and attributes that must be portrayed by anyone who has the Holy Spirit indwelling in him or her.

One fruit of the Spirit you must ask the Holy Spirit to produce in you that will help you overcome temptation, is self control. The fruit of self control is what you need to be able to say no to the flesh and its desires. Self control will help you to take a stand to gratify the Spirit rather than the flesh.

Another fruit of the Spirit that you must ask the Holy Spirit to produce in you is love. Paul admonishes us that the love of God compels us. (2 Corinthians 5:14) If you love God, you will give a second thought before breaking his heart by yielding to the flesh and desires.

The Holy Spirit within produces the character of Christ in us. The Holy Spirit works righteousness and holiness in us. At salvation, righteousness is conferred on us by the finished work of Christ on the cross. Through the help of the Holy Spirit, our human spirit is renewed, worked on and fashioned to become Holy, according to the image of Christ. This is not a quick work, **but a gradual and continuous process;** one that can only happen when we yield to the Holy Spirit.

SPIRIT UPON

The Spirit upon, talks about the power of the Holy Spirit that comes upon a believer, and gives him power to do things beyond the natural. The scripture tell us that on the day of Pentecost, cloven tongues of fire rested on the disciples signifying the coming of the Holy Spirit.

The Spirit upon, is the power of the Holy Spirit that comes to break the yoke of addiction and negative habits in the life of a believer. You cannot break free on your own, but it shall come to pass that **the yoke shall be broken because of the anointing.**

The Spirit upon, is the power of the Holy Spirit that comes to burn away the chaff and debris in our lives, that stands in the way of our true manifestation as believers.

> *"But who can endure the day of His coming? And who*
> *can stand when He appears? For He is like a*
> *refiner's fire and like launderers' soap. He will sit as*
> *a refiner and a purifier of silver; He will purify the*
> *sons of Levi, and purge them as gold and silver,*
> *that they may offer to the Lord an offering in*
> *righteousness."*

MALACHI 3:2-3

It is the Spirit upon that refines and purifies the saint. By the hand of the Holy Spirit upon a believer's life, he becomes fashioned towards holiness and purity.

The Spirit upon is also the power of the Holy Spirit that scriptures describe when it says, "Out of your belly will flow rivers of living waters." It is the hand of the Holy Spirit upon a believer's life that produces the evidence of speaking in new tongues. The believer begins to speak mysteries in the spirit by the help and enablement of the Holy Spirit. As the believer prays in the Holy Spirit, he exchanges weakness for strength, addictions for freedom, inabilities for God's ability.

It is often said, "A man that sins stops praying, and a man that prays stops sinning." Hallelujah, this is what the Holy Spirit can do in us if we yield to him and allow him to work **within and upon us.**

NOTE: There are not two Holy Spirits, the Spirit upon and within talks about two operating points of the Holy Spirit in a believer's life.

You need extra help in order to break free from an addiction, this is because not all addictions are normal, hence **it is only the supernatural ability of the Holy Spirit that can make such deliverance happen.**

word therapy

The word of God is the most powerful and most effective weapon in overcoming the enemy.

The scriptures say, "The word is living and powerful." (Hebrews 4:12). The word of God in your mouth is as powerful as the word of God in God's mouth. God said in the scripture, that He has exalted his word above all his name. (Psalm 138:2). The word of God is Spirit and life. No wonder this weapon is named, "The sword of the Spirit." With it we can fight , avenge and punish all forms of wickedness — only if you have learned "the act of sword fighting".

This means you must learn to know when and where to strike for every situation, crises or challenge we find ourselves in. There is a word of God meant to handle each situation. The same is the case with fighting and overcoming every addiction, negative habit or character flaw. We must find the word of God that suits that predicament and feed it to the situation. As one takes medication twice or thrice a day to handle a health challenge, so we must take dosages of God's word regularly until that spiritual ailment is no more.

No one takes medication on behalf of another, no one can swallow these word pills for you. You must search the scriptures yourselves and swallow the scriptures daily to obtain your healing and deliverance. Daily ingestion of those scriptures and many more, will give you the inner strength and grace to fight and win the battle against temptations and negative habits.

Commit to searching the scripture daily and intentionally for yourself.

Commit to meditating and ingesting the scripture daily for yourself to ensure that your deliverance is perfected.

ELEVEN

accountability and mentorship

As earlier said, one cannot effectively break free from addiction without divine help and physical help. Having discussed the divine help that we need to break free from addictions; this chapter dwells on the physical help that we need to break free from addictions.

On our journey to life, it is important that we know that we cannot and should not walk alone.

A popular quote says,

 "If you want go fast, go alone. If you want to go far, go with someone."

If we must consistently break free from addiction, we must ensure that we submit to accountability and mentorship. We must see to it that we **never walk alone.** This is because **when we go alone, we make ourselves more vulnerable to the devil and his devices.**

Three relationships you must have on life's journey and on your path towards breaking free from addictions include:

1. Mentors
2. Covenant friends
3. Mentees

Mentors: Whatever bondage you are currently struggling with, someone has been there already, has fought it, won it and overcome it. It would only **be wise to find such persons** and submit to their authority. There is a knowledge and an experience that has been given to them which you need to help you successfully overcome. Someone once said, "Experience is the best teacher but I would rather learn from other people's experiences."

I remember the first time that my husband and I met. I didn't know what to expect, as I had never been in such a relationship before. I had to submit to the mentorship of a mother who was not just a spiritual leader, but she also had the necessary experience that I needed, as I prayerfully made the decision that led to my marriage.

Whatever future you hope to build or live in, someone is currently living in it. **Find that person who is living in your future** at the present; connect and submit to their tutelage and guidance and you will get to where you are going… much faster.

Covenant friends: The role of covenant friends on your journey to life cannot be over emphasized. The scriptures clearly say, "There is a friend that sticks closer than a brother." **This is a covenant friend.**

Many persons come into our lives for a season, others for a reason. And this is why you must be spiritually discerning and sensitive to know the who, why, when and where of **every relationship in your life.**

- **Who:** Who is this person in my life and in my journey to destiny?
- **Why:** What is the purpose of our meeting, why did God allow our paths to cross?
- **When:** Why did this person walk into my life in this season of my life? I believe the timing also has a role to play.
- **Where:** The direction of the relationship is also important , so, the question is where are we headed in this relationship?

Every David needs a Jonathan to fulfill his destiny. Hence, if you are struggling with an addiction or character flaw, you need friends of strong character and values, who can hold you by the hand in that season of your life.

They can help to check up on you, remind you to pray and fast, remind you to study, and many other ways. Stay on you to ensure that you don't have space to fall back into your addictions. Even the scriptures say, "Iron sharpens iron." Hence you must prayerfully choose and select friends who would agree to walk with you on your pathway to purity, holiness and fulfillment of purpose.

Mentees: Another group of persons you must walk with on your journey to purity and fulfillment of destiny are mentees. No wonder Jesus' last parting words were "Go and make disciples." (Matthew 28:19) .

I can personally say that discipleship has a way of keeping you on track. When you know that there are lives that are looking up to you, counting on your success and looking to you for encouragement and motivation, that helps you be responsible.

I believe God's pattern to keep believers on track is discipleship. Discipleship follows the principle of rooting (root formation) and fruiting (fruit bearing). We are expected to take root downwards as we keep working on ourselves and dropping every besetting sin and habit. Then we bear fruit upwards by showing evidence of purity and a life of holiness, trusting and serving the Lord. (Isaiah 37:31)

I can personally say that the place of mentees in my life, has helped keep me on track, knowing that my mistakes are not just personal, but generational, as nations are tied to my loins. This is why I personally and gladly accept every invitation to mentor, not because of the title but because it has helped preserve me and the values that I live for.

> The people in your life can make you or mar you, choose wisely.

cured to cure

For every deliverance that God does in your life, there is a higher calling, a higher purpose. **God cured you so you can be a cure to others.** He delivered you from the devil's grip so that you can become the devil's nemesis and worst nightmare.

Your deliverance is perfected in the place of service. God said through Moses to Pharaoh, "Let my people go, that they may serve me." (Exodus 8:1) Hence, the purpose of deliverance is for service.

You must not wait until you are all perfected. Find that person who is laden by the devil the way you were; one that is held and bound by the enemy of their soul, and help the person attain his or her own deliverance.

> By so doing **you will seal your testimony of deliverance.**

MOVING FORWARD

introspection theory

Introspection refers to the act of looking inwards.

A famous philosopher, Aristotle, was popular for his quote, "Man know thyself." No one knows you and should know you better than yourself. Knowing yourself is a strong tool to overcoming addictions, sexual temptations and character flaws.

If you know that visiting him alone turns on all the wires inside of you, then you should not be caught visiting him alone. Rather you should go with a covenant friend, meet in public places, ask him for a visit to your place instead, especially when the rest of your family are present. This way you put out the fire even before it starts.

 Don't fuel your passions, water them.

substitution theory

Jesus Christ said in the scriptures, that when a demon is cast out if nothing occupies its former house, it comes back to check, and the second time it comes back with seven more demons worse than itself. The last state of that man is worse than first. (Matthew 12:44-45)

This truth revealed by our Lord Jesus Christ in the scriptures proves that **nature abhors a vacuum.**

Thus, if you want to truly be free from that addiction, temptation and character flaw, **then you must be ready to replace the unwanted with the wanted and stick to it until the wanted becomes your new habit.**

When I was younger, I once struggled with masturbation, and one thing I realized was that the urge to commit this sin often came when I was alone. And so, most times I desired to be alone to day dream and fantasize. This opened my mind to the oppression of the dirty demon responsible for this addiction.

After the Holy Spirit worked on me, and I started my journey towards my deliverance and freedom, I decided that I would not stay alone especially in the evenings. If I was alone, I chose to substitute the day dreaming and fantasies for worship and study of the word in the evenings. Gradually, I became free.

The Bible in Philippians 4:8 tells us to "Think on these things." 'These things' means that we are expected to substitute negative thought patterns for positive ones.

> Dear reader, you know yourself, you know what should go from your life. Apply the introspection theory and look within. Then you can carefully substitute and make the necessary changes to your thought patterns, habits, values and life in totality.

reward theory

Everyone has a special treat that leaves the feeling of appreciation in them. As we travel on our journey towards breaking addictions and becoming better persons, we must take some time to appreciate our little efforts and thriving, enabled by the Spirit of God. We must learn to be grateful, celebrate and appreciate the grace of God in our lives that was not in vain. (1 Corinthians 15:10)

The flesh loves to be indulged and pampered, but we must not indulge our flesh. Rather, as we successfully break free from these addictions and negative habits, please feel free to celebrate and treat yourself. This will serve as encouragement and motivation to keep living and doing right by the help and enablement of the Spirit of God.

Dear reader, rather than let the enemy of your soul celebrate over your downfall and fallen state, receive grace from the Spirit of God to live right and boldly celebrate your little wins. **"For though the righteous may fall seven times, and rise again."** (Proverbs 24:16).

Keep in mind that the reward system is not to get you relaxed and feeling as one who has attained, rather it is a motivation to press towards the mark for the high calling of God in Christ Jesus. (Philippians 3:14) .

elimination theory

In the scripture, Jesus said that if our right hand causes us to sin, we must cut it off and cast it from us. (Matthew 5:30) Hence, whatever fuels or encourages that addiction, temptation and character flaw, we must learn to take the bull by its horns and do the needful.

We must flee.

Paul said in the scripture that "all things are lawful for me, but all things are not helpful, all things are lawful for me, but not all things edify". (1 Corinthians 10:23)

We must therefore strive to do away with those things in our lives that are not helpful for our growth, development and walk with God.

Don't just sit and pray for deliverance, take the drastic measure and apologize later if need be. If you need to cut off from the wrong friends, stop watching a TV program... just do the needful. If you know that hanging out with some friends leaves you feeling dirty, but also longing to fulfill lustful desires. Then my friend, you must end such relationship and company. At one time in my early youthful years, I had to ban myself from looking at a television or movie screen for 3 months, until I was sure that my mind was completely cleared of the toxins resulting from what I had watched over time.

The impurities that pollute our mind, soul and body comes from the outside and hence, we must guard our gates. Every human being has gates (access points into his or her mind, body and soul). These gates include; the ear gate, eye gate, sexual organs gate, the forehead and mouth gate. We must learn to guard these gates to preserve our soul from the oppression of the devil and his demons. Which is often seen in addictions, demonic possession, sexual temptations and perversions.

The scriptures say that if dross is taken away from silver it will go to the silversmith for jewelry. (Proverbs 25:4)

Dear reader if you can eliminate the unhelpful and unnecessary habits and addictions in your life, you will be fit and ready to travel on the journey of purpose and destiny. Scriptures also say that we should lay aside every weight and the sin that easily besets us, seeing that we are surrounded by a great cloud of witnesses.

 It is time to travel LIGHT so we can get to our destination.

Make that decision today, do away with the excess baggage of guilt and shame from falling into temptation...

...**and your joy will be full.**

commitment form

I _____ declare that Jesus Christ is my Lord and Savior.

I declare today_____ that sin shall no longer have dominion over me.

I declare that I am no longer bound to _____ addiction/character flaw.

I declare that I am free to live in purity and wholeness. Not by might or power but by God's Spirit.

I am committed to working out my salvation and deliverance with fear and trembling.

I commit to living out the fruit of the Holy Spirit, so that men may see and glorify my Father in Heaven.

I know it may not be easy, but I declare that I can do all things through Christ who gives me strength.

I commit to be accountable to_____ _____ on my journey towards true and complete freedom.

I commit to loving the Holy Spirit daily, as he leads on my journey.

Signed _____

Date _____

Congratulations. If you have made this commitment feel free to drop us a line at Pillar Girlie on Facebook and we will be happy to pray with you.

about the author

Sandra Alanwoko Lawrence is a passionate social worker with years of experience working with her nonprofit, Pillar-Girl Foundation and other nonprofit organizations.

She has counseled and worked with many young person's dealing with addictions and character issues in rural areas and small towns.

She put together this book to provide practical steps to emerging victorious in the face of addictions and temptations. Sandra is married to Lawrence Inyang and they are blessed with their son Judah.

Find us on Facebook @ Pillar Girlie
facebook.com/pillargirl

www.ingramcontent.com/pod-product-compliance
Lightning Source LLC
Chambersburg PA
CBHW070943120626
46546CB00004B/1547